The Complete
Air Guitar
Handbook

The Complete Air Guitar Handbook

By John McKenna and Michael Moffitt

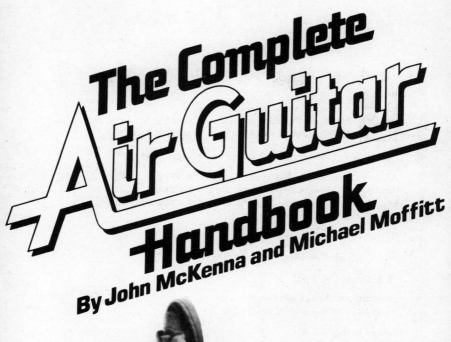

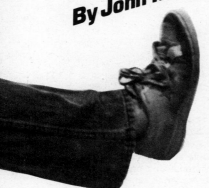

LONG SHADOW BOOKS
PUBLISHED BY POCKET BOOKS NEW YORK

Another *Original* publication of LONG SHADOW BOOKS

A Long Shadow Book published by
POCKET BOOKS, a division of Simon & Schuster, Inc.
1230 Avenue of the Americas, New York, N.Y. 10020

ISBN: 0-671-49677-8

First Long Shadow Books printing November, 1983

10 9 8 7 6 5 4 3 2 1

Long Shadow Books and colophon are
trademarks of Simon & Schuster, Inc.

Printed in the U.S.A.

Design by Jacques Chazaud

Contents

1. *Something in the Air*

In 1956, a young Hoboken lad was playing his parents' hi-fi in the living room while his mother was out shopping. The record was "Blue Suede Shoes" by Elvis Presley, and the volume was turned up as far as it could go. Just the other night he had seen Elvis on "The Ed Sullivan Show" and couldn't believe how great he was. As he sat there in his papa's favorite overstuffed chair, staring at the record as it spun on the turntable, a strange thing started to happen. His eyes began to glaze over. His arms and legs started to twitch involuntarily. His pelvis gyrated in a way he had never even known existed until he saw "The King." Suddenly, a remarkable transformation overcame him. As he heard "The King" wail, "Well it's three to get ready and four to go," he could stand it no longer. He jumped up out of the chair, leaped onto the dining room table, and mimicked with complete accuracy every move he had seen Elvis make. No longer was he a lonely, overweight, acne-pocked adolescent. He *was* "The King." The television lights were blinding him; sweat poured from his body; the hysterical shrieks of hundreds of overwrought teenage girls deafened him.

The first air guitar was born.

With the "British Invasion" of the early sixties, rock music became dominated by the electric guitar. This necessitated the creation of the electric air guitar or "air axe," as it is affectionately called. Subsequently, it developed into the precision instrument we use now, allowing complete versatility for all applications by today's demanding air guitarists.

The vanguard of the British groups, such as the Beatles, the Rolling Stones, and the Dave Clark Five, delivered popular music tailor-made to air guitaring. The words were simple, easily memorized, and easily mimed. But, best of all, the music was rhythmic, the beat was strong, and the lead guitar breaks were simple—a perfect combination for the air guitarist. The air guitar as a cult phenomenon had arrived!

Unfortunately, this arrival met with neither total, nor reasonable, acceptance. Air guitarists were arrested, jailed, and sometimes institutionalized. Whether their frenzied motion was a sort of seizure, or perhaps a rebellious ritual, or even total lunacy—whatever the cause, the air guitarists were, at least, disturbing the peace, so they were persecuted. This near total misinterpretation of air guitaring resulted in the formation of the legendary "air underground." Until the end of the decade, dedicated air guitarists withdrew to their homes and hideaways to play to the tunes of the Byrds, the Hollies, the Lovin' Spoonful, and the Buffalo Springfield, among others. Air guitarists practiced and played faithfully, avoiding the public eye, until the mood of the times would change and air guitaring could be enjoyed openly for what it really is—a clean, safe way to bring the fantasy of rock 'n' roll stardom to everyone.

In the seventies, the heavy metal bands prospered on the rock scene. Long guitar solos and the dominance of the rhythm guitar were the order of the day. Air guitar techniques advanced out of the stone age and air guitarists came out of hiding. More and more air guitarists would show off at parties, dances and bars. They started to gravitate toward each other. Phone numbers were exchanged, which led to the first air bands. People started to specialize in air singing, lead, rhythm and bass air guitars, air piano and even air drums. These first crude air bands had more raw energy than talent, but those who stuck with their training have become the legendary Air Masters of today.

Guitarists from this era such as Pete Townshend and Keith Richard demonstrated the energy and vigor necessary to play commanding lead guitar. Air guitarists thrived on their hard-driving music and on-stage gymnastics. The rock stage became a circus where the performers constantly tried to outdo themselves and each other. Mick Jagger, Roger Daltrey, and Rod Stewart provided a showcase for the air vocalist. You didn't need an instrument anymore—you could dash, leap, and strut with only a microphone (and now, an *air* microphone!).

If theatrics were your "bag," performers like Kiss and Alice Cooper inspired air guitarists and vocalists alike. The appropriate costume, album, and air instrument could propel anyone onto centerstage at a party, in a bar or classroom.

The mid-seventies witnessed the rise of stars such as Bruce Springsteen and Tom Petty. Like Chuck Berry some twenty years earlier, these performers were "triple threats"— they wrote their own songs, sang the lead vocals, and played lead guitar. More than ever, the air performer could be the consummate artist himself.

In the eighties, the new crop of air guitarists and air musicians coming out of high schools and colleges, coupled with the Air Masters, have brought this art to a new peak. The high visibility of air guitaring, thanks to increased press coverage, has caused air band contests to become incredibly competitive. Air Masters are in great demand to hold clinics for aspiring air bands.

A definitive manual on the state of the art is long overdue. And while we are well aware of the limitations of trying to teach anything as subtle as air guitaring from a mere book, we nevertheless feel it is worth a try.

If you follow the advice in this book, you will be well on the way to becoming a legend in your own mind.

2. Get to Know Your Instrument

Remember that the air guitar has size and shape. With most novices you can't tell if they are playing a ukulele or a tuba. Most air guitars are designed for rock 'n' roll use, and therefore, are electric. While the specific shape may vary greatly, most electric air guitars are between thirty-six and forty-six inches in length, with a width of about fourteen to eighteen inches at the widest point. The most popular models have solid or semi-acoustic bodies, varying in depth

Electric Air Guitar

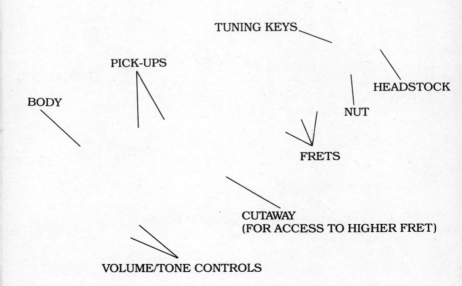

from two to four inches. The electronics differ from model to model, with most having two pick-ups and three or four control knobs. (These knobs are adjusted to attain desirable volume and tone.)

Although most of the pointers in this book refer to air axes, the original, prototype air guitar was acoustic. The length and width of these acoustic instruments are slightly greater than the more streamlined electrics, and the depth is usually four to six inches. They are still used on occasion, so air guitarists should have at least one acoustic instrument available for any "folksy," country, or rockabilly songs in their repertoires.

Acoustic Air Guitar

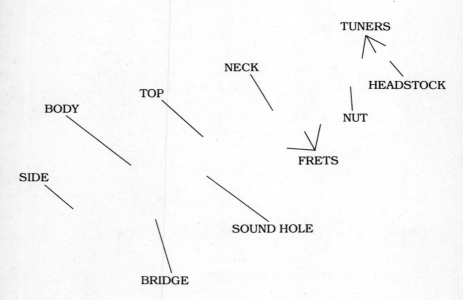

3. Correct Positioning of the Air Guitar

To hold the air pick, place it between the index finger and the thumb of the right hand and close the thumb on the index finger. Play a chord by striking downward on the imaginary strings with the main movement coming from the wrist. As your confidence grows, the arm may be used more to accent certain chords.

While you are strumming with the right hand, the left hand executes the chord variations dictated by the song. There is no need to learn actual chord variations and music theory. The only thing you must, we repeat, *must* remember is this: the lower the notes, the closer you play to the head stock of the guitar. The higher the notes, the closer into the body of the guitar you play. It looks very silly to be playing in the wrong direction.

How high you wear the guitar is also of paramount concern. Today most real guitarists are either "gunslingers" or "semi-gunslingers." A gunslinger wears the guitar real low and strums at hip level. The semi-gunslinger wears the guitar set to strum no more than halfway between the hip and the navel. Wear the guitar any higher and you'll look like Tommy Smothers (and no one wants to look like that).

Left-Handed vs. Right-Handed

There is no stigma to playing the guitar left-handed in today's rock scene. Several of the most famous guitarists, such as Jimi Hendrix and Paul McCartney, have been left-handed. In jamming with right-handed guitarists, however, the necks of the instruments tend to collide. So please stay to the right side of any right-handed guitarists. That way you'll avoid hitting each other in the head with your instruments.

Gunslinger

Semi-Gunslinger

BB Gunslinger

Right-Handed Stance

Left-Handed Stance

Tuning

The easiest and quickest way to tune an air guitar is by getting it in pitch with an air piano or organ. Since these instruments rarely get out of tune, we recommend that the novice air guitarist use this method.

4. Extra Equipment

As you get into playing the air guitar, there are certain additional pieces of equipment that you may want to have.

Air Amplifiers

The air amplifier has become very common among the best air guitarists. Ever since Dylan "went electric," the need for power has increased. Turning the volume control on your air amp to the proper level in conjunction with your stereo volume control will maximize the impression that you know what you're doing.

Air Amp

Air amps are available in various shapes, sizes, and power ratings. (The amp shown here is a 200 watt, dual-channel model with separate controls for volume, tone, treble, and bass.) As illustrated, a wall socket is necessary as a source of power; in remote locations use of extremely long air extension cords is advisable.

Air Mikes

The air mike is a must for anyone who intends to take center stage at a performance. It doesn't matter if you can't sing a note—just make sure that you *memorize all the words* and can pretend to sing them. If you can't remember all the words just mimic the chorus of the song. If you can't even do that, then keep your mouth shut or you'll look like a jerk.

Air Mike

This air mike is the unidirectional, hand-held model preferred by most lead singers. For increased onstage mobility, wireless mikes are available. Either type can be used with a mike stand when necessary.

Foot Switches

The foot switch has been gaining in popularity among today's high-powered guitarists. Its function is to boost the sound level during lead breaks in order to accent the guitar over the other instruments. All you have to do is step on the foot switch just before the solo. The switch is usually placed just to the right of the air mike stand on the floor. Step on the foot switch with authority so everyone knows you are taking charge. After your wonderful solo, casually step on the switch to turn it down, as you nonchalantly blend back into the band. It has a great affect on audiences. They see, just from these little things, how classy you really are. Remember you are trying to give the illusion that you are actually *playing* the music. Even the smallest detail is noticed by your fans.

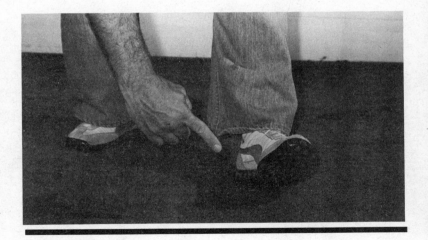

Foot Switch

The foot switch shown here has fuzz-tone and wah-wah capabilities. Virtually any electronic effect is possible with today's air foot switches.

Air Drums

Every air band needs an air drummer to round things out. The only equipment that an air drummer needs is a chair—preferably a kitchen chair—or anything without arms. An inverted wastebasket or bucket is fine also.

There is a major controversy over the use of real drum sticks while playing the air drums. We feel using drum sticks helps the overall effect of pounding out that savage beat.

Maintenance

The above items need very little maintenance. Make sure that they are kept clean, and you'll have years of trouble-free pleasure from your equipment.

Air Drummer Going at It

A concrete block provides a convenient seat for this air drummer. Drumsticks and a double bass drum setup are, of course, optional.

5. Clothing

Headgear

Rock guitar superstars Jimi Hendrix and Keith Richard have paved the way for the wearing of the bandana. It dates back to the "pirate days of yore" which the present-day rock stars try to emulate. It is also useful in keeping perspiration out of the eyes, and after ten minutes of performance you should be sweating pretty heavily if you are playing with any enthusiasm at all. In addition to bandanas, sweatbands and wristbands are also making inroads with well-dressed air guitarists.

The cowboy hat is appropriate when playing in a country or Southern rock band but not when performing to AC/DC. The same applies to wearing a baseball hat. It's cool when performing Cheap Trick but not for other bands.

T-shirts

Currently, the most acceptable upper body wear is the T-shirt. Wearing a concert shirt of the artist you are listening to is considered chic. The older the shirt the better. For example, the Rolling Stones tour shirts from 1975 are more desirable than the 1981 shirts. They give the impression that you have been "with the band" for a long time. Another option in this vein is to copy the "look" of the band (or particular band member) you are mimicking. For example, Keith Richard, as the consummate Rolling Stone, adopts varied wardrobe changes—from Victorian ruffled shirts to an evil satanic leather vest. Just take your pick—he does.

Torn shorts or sleeveless shirts have become the trademark of new wave and punk bands, and they are acceptable only with related musical performances.

Acceptable Clothing:

**Concert T-shirt
Regular jeans
Backstage pass**

Unacceptable Clothing:

*Golf shirt
Designer pants
He's playing toilet paper*

The shirtless look is a popular one. Shirtless air guitarists often perform at outdoor concerts, beach parties or (seasonally) at home. While practicing, the shirtless performer is unencumbered, not only in movement but also in his choice of music—he can switch from album to album, artist to artist, without time-consuming wardrobe changes.

Shirtless air guitarists, however, have a tendency to turn their minds over to the wonders of modern chemistry or to flood their systems with alcoholic antifreeze. We then call them "faced." Donning nothing more than a pair of jeans, these aspiring virtuosos brave all types of weather to make appearances at every possible concert. Though glassy-eyed and unsure of foot, the "faced" air guitarist has earned his place in our hearts and this book.

As you can see, musical preference and personal taste dictate shirtwear; however, basic rational guidelines must be observed. Turtlenecks are gauche. And no golf shirts, please—even when performing to the Beach Boys. This is a definite no-no.

"Faced" Air Guitarist

Since performances by "faced" air guitarists are, by nature, spontaneous and brief, action photos are rare. This air guitarist has just completed a frenzied, short-lived set, and is shown here preparing for his encore performance.

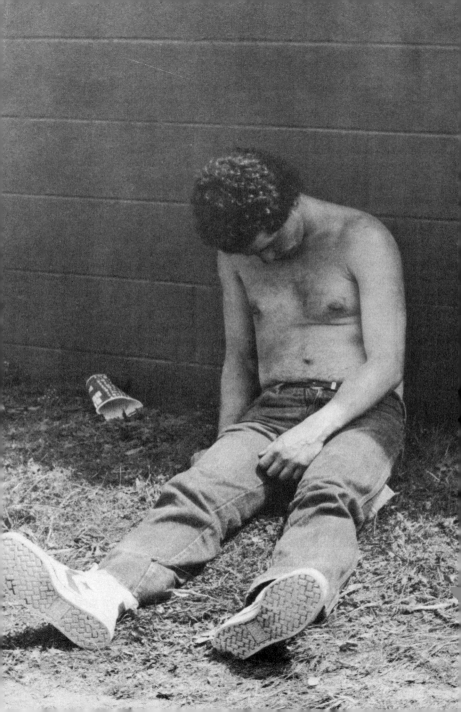

Jackets

For traveling to and from your next gig, cooler weather may dictate outerwear such as a jacket. Of course, the only kind that is permissible under any circumstances is a tour jacket. Tour jackets are styled along the lines of baseball warm-up jackets. They usually have a nylon outer shell with the name and logo of the band on the back. On the front some even have a small logo over the left breast. Rock magazines generally offer tour jackets of currently popular groups, while the rare jackets might take some ingenuity to acquire.

Tour Jackets

The air guitarists shown here are on tour (note air guitar travel kit). The tour jackets reflect their respective tastes in music.

Pants

Many people will argue, but we feel the only pants to wear for heavy-duty air guitaring are jeans. Levis or Lees are recommended, never designer jeans. Designer jeans try to impress, but true air guitarists do not have to impress anyone—as a matter of fact, if they did want to impress someone they would be playing *real* guitars. We must also be adamant about avoiding spandex pants. Leather pants are OK, but never spandex. Jimi Hendrix and Jim Morrison would turn over in their graves if they knew one of their emulators ever wore spandex.

As everyone knows, a backstage pass is *the* badge worn only by the band and road crew. Recently a new brand of jeans was introduced called "BackStagePass Jeans." They really fit the bill for the connoisseur air guitarist. On the right leg just above the knee is a facsimile of a backstage pass used at many of today's rock concerts.

Authors' note: While the "T-shirts" section discussed the shirtless option, we don't condone going *pantless!* Be advised this practice is not only dangerous indoors, but illegal outdoors. You have been warned.

Footwear

Comfort is all important, especially if you are planning to play for a long period of time. Most air guitarists we know prefer sneakers or athletic shoes to give traction, as a lot of the movements required during a performance tend to be athletic in nature.

Those who depend on a heavy foot stomping in their acts prefer the boot—either cowboy or "Beatle boots" or variations on this theme. Most rock performers tend to wear boots, but ultimately the choice is yours.

Jeans with a Backstage Pass

Playing barefoot is advisable only when practicing around the house. There are fewer hazards indoors, and your footing is much more predictable in familiar surroundings. Unless you're at the beach, usually the only barefoot air guitarists you'll see are completely "faced" (as mentioned earlier in "T-shirts"). They are unaware of their *feet* so they could care less about footwear.

6. *Where to Play*

The vast majority of your practicing and playing time will be spent at home, so careful attention should be given to your living arrangements. The use of rooms, space, and furniture are therefore extremely important.

Many air guitarists live with their parents. Usually this situation limits air guitar playing to the guitarist's bedroom. No sweat. Just sell your bed. This will amply increase your performance area, and the money obtained can be applied toward headphones (with a long cord) or perhaps a sleeping bag. When you dispose of the bed, merely inform your parents that when you cleaned up your room you couldn't find it. Being familiar with your room they will: 1)believe you, 2)be happy you finally cleaned it, and 3)inform you that until you take better care of your belongings they will not buy you another bed. Fine. You are ready to practice.

Air Guitarist's Bedroom

This air guitarist has sold his mattress and adjusted his box springs to provide a private, spacious area in which to practice. Mirrors are placed strategically to view technique.

The family room (or Florida room) is another choice area for air guitaring. The stereo is nearby, the furniture is more mobile, and you're probably far enough from the front door so you won't be interrupted by uninvited visitors.

The living room-dining room area is fine for play and practice, but these rooms usually contain more expensive and breakable items. Replacement costs and sentimental value are much more sobering when you're surveying the damage the morning after than during the fervor of playing the night before. So regulate your movements accordingly.

Playing the air guitar in the shower and bath often either accompanies or replaces traditional bathroom singing. This is an unfortunate, dangerous activity. The hazards involved in air guitarists' movements in a wet tub or shower are all too obvious and the resultant accidents have provoked several state legislatures to seek laws completely banning air guitar playing in bathrooms. We are against government interference in our activities, so please don't fuel their legal fires by becoming a statistic!

The air guitarist who has his own house or apartment is the king of his castle and can utilize rooms, hallways, and furniture as he deems fit. However, any apartment-dwelling air guitarist should situate himself (relocating if necessary) in a ground-floor apartment. The hopping, jumping, and sliding which are crucial to most performances will not be tolerated by tenants living below.

Air Guitarist's Living Room

A parent and creative air guitar practice are generally considered mutually exclusive. This fledgling air guitarist attempted too much too soon in his parents' living room. He's now an orphan.

Many fledgling air guitarists are found in colleges and universities around the country. The average dormitory room has enough floor space for rudimentary air guitar movements. Bunkbeds save space and cheap college-issue desks are easily moved around. However, the success of your playing *completely* depends on the acceptance of your peers. Your roommate can be won over, not only to acceptance but to energetic participation. Most students today are well aware that studying and grades are unimportant, while peer acceptance is the foundation for a normal, happy life. Again, though, no playing in the bathroom. Dorm bathrooms are usually communal setups, so physical hazards are compounded geometrically. We won't even go into the possibilities of indelible humiliation.

With the exception of "partying" (which we will cover later in this book) the above paragraph also applies to occupants of fraternity and sorority houses.

7. Stereo Equipment

Book after book has been written on the quality of this piece of equipment vs. that piece. Well, we do not intend to get into that subject here, but we do have several basic ideas about sound systems.

1. Amplifier

Whether you go into separates or a receiver it is mandatory that you have at least 70 watts RMS per channel or you ain't gonna rock nothin'. We are currently using 100 watts per channel and that is definitely not enough. So the word here is POWER with a capital "P." We don't care if you have to sell your first-born child or knock off Fort Knox, but you got to have a lot of juice.

2. Speakers

Just make sure they have the ability to handle the power you put through them. Here individual taste and pocketbook come into play. Don't be fooled by some razzmatazz that the stereo salesman puts on you (John should know, he sold stereos for over a year just so he could practice playing the air guitar all day). Remember, bring an album that you really know with you and ask the salesman to play it. Make sure you position yourself between the salesman and the volume control of the amp being used. The reason for this is obvious. The salesman won't turn the amp up loud enough for true testing under concert-like conditions so you must take control of the place. Don't worry about the salesman. He's too worried about losing a sale to do anything to stop you. Just make sure you can get those speakers to the sound level you desire. If they don't measure up to your standards, there are always other speaker shops and other salesmen. Personally, we enjoy watching that cocky smirk slip off the salesman's face once you crank up the box!

3. Turntables, Accessories, etc.

These items aren't important enough to cover in this book, because we want to get on with it.

4. Headphones

They have definitely prevented many evictions and have allowed individuals to carry on without infringing on others' sound space.

5. Tape Deck

Since even the finest tone arms jump out of the groove during energetic performances, a tape deck is a very important addition to your home entertainment center. Rather than having to waste time changing records, we suggest you make two or three ninety-minute tapes of your favorite songs with those special lead guitar riffs, so you can jump from one song to the next without missing a beat.

The next question you must ask concerns the type of tape deck: 8-track, open reel, or cassette. Well, forget the 8-track altogether. The real discussion concerns the cassette vs. the open reel. We opt for the cassette for the sake of convenience. You might also like to run through your routines mentally in the privacy of your car as you cruise to and fro.

Going Mobile

If you own a car you *must*, we repeat *must*, have a good system. As the earth gets more and more populated, it gets harder and harder to find a good space in which to get down. The car is a great place to memorize the guitar solos which are crucial in this increasingly competitive form of entertainment.

Whenever we travel, which is often, we run into the problem of practicing and jamming while away. Since it's not practical to drag around several hundred pounds of hi-fi gear and albums, we've devised the Air Guitarist's Travel Kit. This

Air Guitar Travel Kit

The owner of this travel kit has opted for the Walkman tape player and a mixed selection of music. The mirror is indispensable.

kit includes all the basic necessities. In an attache case (eventually covered with backstage passes) are the following items: a portable cassette player with ample tapes, an air guitar, an 8 x 11 inch mirror (for watching performances) and several air guitar picks. This kit is with us at all times, whether we go on long trips or just down to the local store, because you never know when the urge may hit.

Not enough data are in so far on the Sony Walkman, but the tests are very encouraging. It offers the convenience of headphones but has the portability that conventional equipment does not have. The Walkman provides total freedom of movement and thus many more opportunities to play the air guitar than were imaginable even a year ago.

We see only two drawbacks to these units: they are too fragile for many of the really physical air guitarists, and they eliminate interaction between two or more air guitarists. But they definitely come in handy on the road.

Air Guitarist Using a Walkman

This guitarist goes mobile with his Walkman. This particular unit also includes an AM-FM radio.

8. Safety for Beginners

The true Air Master must have the grace of a ballerina, the stamina of a long-distance runner, the expressiveness of a mime, the confidence of a matador, and the controlled abandon of a downhill racer. Fortunately, all of these can be attained (or at least strived for) by anyone with the brains of a begonia. Ergo, we feel compelled to stress our concern for safety.

You, the aspiring air guitarist, should "let your fingers do the walking" into (and through) the yellow pages of your local phone book. Not only does this provide exercise for your dexterous digits, but when combined with nominal eye-hand coordination and a functional knowledge of the alphabet, you will arrive at the listing for "Sporting Goods—Retail." Peruse the listings, find the most convenient sporting goods store, and go visit it.

Authors' note: we must recommend visits *during* the store's business hours. While an after-hours visit may provide considerable monetary savings, prison is no place to learn to play the air guitar. Please use cash or a credit card, and *buy* the necessary items.

These items are mandatory:

> Everything humanly available to outfit a
> professional hockey player. Everything.

Ice skates provide valuable ankle support, and the balance required to function in skates will prove indispensable later on. Get used to them, so that any later challenge on

---

The Properly Prepared Novice

This aspiring air guitarist has appropriately outfitted himself for a safe and enthusiastic entry into the world of air guitar stardom.

normal (or treacherous) footing will be met and conquered with ease.

Moving up the body we find shin protectors and knee pads. Again, these are a *must*. Inconsiderate parents, friends, and roommates are always leaving obstacles in the fledgling air guitarist's path. So, watch out! Knee pads also provide necessary protection for perilous knee drops and running knee slides. They should be worn until thick callouses have developed on the knees.

Hip protectors and athletic cups (males only) are next. Every athlete knows how painful a "hip pointer" can be; we're not exactly sure what one is, but don't find out the hard way—wear those hip pads. The hip protectors can be discarded when your progress allows.

Safety equipment for the torso includes rib and kidney protectors. Do not be too quick, however, to give up this equipment. Confidence is wonderful, but pain hurts. Basic, but true.

Shoulder pads should be worn by all beginners until the basics have been conquered, especially whenever another beginning air guitarist is in the same room. Correct that—in the same *building*.

The outer garments for hockey are loose-fitting and comfortable. They allow free movement for any part of the body and will prove most comfortable for air guitar practice long after other beginners' apparel has been shed.

The hockey stick itself, although not necessary, is strongly recommended as practice equipment. Its shape and dimensions make it a perfect air guitar substitute. Once the novice has the basic grip and a feel for the stick, he may discard it in favor of the air guitar itself. However, while practicing and wearing the beginner's protective equipment, it is a good idea to keep the hockey stick within reach. If anyone (a parent, sibling, or friend) should interrupt a practice session, the air guitarist can just mumble something about "dropping my stick while firing that last slap shot." A further cursory explanation about "trying out for the 1984 US olympic ice hockey team" may be necessary as well. But this slight embarrassment is trivial compared to the total humiliation you might feel standing there dressed like "The Great Gretzky," no hockey stick in sight, and "Bad Moon Rising" blaring out of your stereo. Besides, the stick is very handy for swatting away any unwanted intruders.

Finally, we arrive at headgear. The hockey helmet is fine; it protects the top, back and sides of the head. However, due to the unpredictability of novice air guitarists' movements, we suggest protection for the face, also. Table corners, lamps, stereos, and TV's prove to be very unforgiving obstacles during a mishap. Buy a football helmet. With a big mask. You'll thank yourself later.

Keep pockets clean, and remove any encumbering clothing (e.g., loose straps, key chains, or straight jackets). Whatever the situation, be aware of your surroundings. A perfectly executed "Flying Springsteen" is worthless if you land on your mother's poodle! Keep all pets and small children secured elsewhere. In fact, we've had considerable luck just letting pets and kids loose outside, then notifying parents that they're gone. (Not only does this clear the house of little annoyances, but larger ones as well—if you see what we mean!) Anyway, be aware of your surroundings and stay alert. Dozens of teenage deaths each year result from unsafe air guitar practices. Air guitaring, fortunately, has not received a bad name due to these fatalities, since most of them are recorded as bizarre suicides or unexplained accidents. But *don't* be a statistic—be careful!

9. Air Guitar Substitutes

You may find it helpful to use a tangible air guitar substitute when practicing a difficult leap, slide, or other movement. While many household items are adequate, the tennis racquet is the most widely used. Its general shape and dimensions, along with its durability and light weight, give the player a genuine feel for the instrument. Other acceptable items include a hockey stick, a yardstick, a baseball bat, a T-square, or simply a 2 x 4 piece of wood. If a real guitar is available, that's fine too—but, unless you know how to play the real thing, you may get discouraged quickly if you accidentally strum or pick the strings.

Other substitutes are not only ill-conceived, but downright dangerous. Basketballs, for instance, prove unwieldy as air guitar substitutes. It is also advisable *not* to use small babies or household pets; that could prove to be a traumatic experience for them *and* you. Chain saws should *never* be used. Although their dimensions are suitable, they are generally too heavy (and there are already enough people in the world who are nicknamed "Lefty"). Unless you absolutely *must,* we also discourage the use of firearms (such as shotguns, rifles, etc.). Even Wendy O. Williams fans should steer clear of this type of practice tool.

Whatever your choice of air guitar substitute, exercise good judgment, caution, and discretion. Even though many air guitar contests consider tennis racquets acceptable, the true purist hones his talents solely toward the use of an *air* instrument.

Air Guitar Practice Substitutes

Acceptable	*Unacceptable*
real electric & acoustic guitars	grand pianos
brooms	Hoover vacuums
tennis racquets	tennis balls
hockey sticks	hockey pucks
T-squares	Mr. T
baseball bats	vampire bats
bowling pins	bowling balls
2 × 4's	8 × 8's

Acceptable Air Guitar Substitutes

Tennis racquet   ***Broomstick***
                            (à la Jimi Hendrix)

Unacceptable
Air Guitar Substitute

Chain saw

10. Practice

Now that you've finished practicing with a substitute, you're ready for the big leagues. Put down your tennis racquet, hockey stick, broom, 2 x 4 or mother, and pick up your air guitar.

Getting in Shape

The best way to get in shape for an air guitar contest is simply to practice every day. The people who think that jazzercise will get them in shape have never tried rock-o-cise. It stimulates your cardiovascular system and develops your arm and leg muscles. When they carry Springsteen off the stage on a stretcher after three and a half hours of playing, you'll know just how he feels.

When to Do It

The serious air guitarist trains in excess of three hours a day. Most feel that the evening is the best time. But since the constant thumping and pounding disturb the faint of heart, apartment complexes often frown on this. Altering one's training period to accommodate neighbors is often a wise idea.

We practice an hour every morning, with a two-hour, heavy "get-down" session in the evening. The morning session should start with the most basic repetitions. You can also do your experimenting then because you're not likely to have an audience. You should consider the evening session a live performance where you can strut your stuff. Evening performances should be given with all the zest that the top rock performers exhibit in their stage shows. Try to have every note on key, every word exact and every lead break look passionate. The guitar and the player should be as one, joined together as only a musician and his instrument can be.

As in many athletic endeavors, training with others is often a good idea. It gives you the opportunity to compete on a friendly basis and actually makes some of the more grueling "breaks" a lot more cohesive. Even Jimi Hendrix worked with other musicians.

Warming Up

The fingers are important in playing and should be warmed up accordingly. The hand to concentrate on is the hand which will be holding the neck of the guitar. This would be the left hand in a right-handed position and vice versa. The conditioning of this hand is crucial because it must shape, hold, and control every chord you play, *plus* locate, bend, and (if necessary) vibrate every note you play. We recommend that a drumming motion involving all fingers be applied at least thirty minutes of every waking hour. Simply drum or tap your fingers on your desk at school or work, on your leg or dashboard as you drive. It is a simple yet invaluable exercise that keeps your fingers in shape and adds credibility and finesse to your playing.

Looking Good

Now that you are thoroughly warmed up it is time to put on your opening number. Turn on the old stereo and gently work into a medium-tempo song—nothing too heavy or complicated. Just try to imagine walking on stage and concentrate on the music. Work up to the more difficult parts as you get further into the routine. After about six or seven numbers you should be loose enough to start getting fancy.

Many advanced air guitarists use audience overdubbed tapes to give them that extra drive. You can get this effect by tinkering a little with a tape deck. Bring the record level up on the deck while recording applause from any live album, then bring it down to zero just before the song begins. Tape any studio version of your music and repeat the applause afterwards. With a little practice this method of taping is very effective and you'll really believe you just stepped on stage at Madison Square Garden.

11. The Stage

Many air guitarists go to great pains to set up the stage area properly. One Air Master we know has what we consider the ultimate stage set up in his living room. Unfortunately, he would not let us photograph it. We respect his privacy but will try to explain his layout.

The "front" wall of his stage is a mural of the audience at Woodstock as seen from the stage. So what you view is hundreds of thousands of people yelling and clapping for you on stage. It definitely sets the proper mood.

The two side walls are panelled floor to ceiling with mirrors; out of the corners of your eyes you can see the reflection of all your moves on stage.

Naturally, the rear wall of "The Stage" is covered by stereo equipment. Four of the biggest speakers we have ever seen are stacked in each corner. Between these speakers along the rear wall are floor-to-ceiling shelves stocked with all of the latest "state of the art" sound equipment, including two cassette decks and two reel-to-reel recorders. Also on this back wall is an album collection that would be the envy of any radio station. Jammed into the shelves are a twenty-five inch color TV, video recorder and camera setup, which enable him to videotape his training session.

When you crank up the stereo through those huge speakers, and look out on to the "Woodstock crowd" you cannot help but get overwhelmed by this scene. It is the ultimate.

We know that most air guitarists are on a more moderate budget, but we just wanted you to understand to what great lengths some air guitarists will go to obtain perfection.

12. The Eight Best Movies for Studying Technique

Now that we have covered training methods, let's talk technique. The best way to learn to be a star is by viewing live and taped performances of the top guitarists in the music world. We personally have a videotape of a Stones concert that we watch at least once a week. Keith Richard has moves that defy description. We still don't know how he does it. Midnight shows at your local theater are also good for research, but beware of faced air guitarists lying in the aisles. The best movies are:

1. *Woodstock.* A classic film. The various artists perform some of their finest work. Alvin Lee is at his best in the song "Goin Home." We cannot say enough about Jimi Hendrix's performance. He lets it all hang out. Pete Townshend was pivotal in showing us that there is more to a guitar than just playing it. And the smashing of his instrument is most enjoyable. This movie also includes the first filmed footage of an air guitarist (namely Joe Cocker).

2. *The Kids Are Alright.* An in–depth look at the Who. Any air guitarist must see Townshend at his peak.

3. *Song Remains the Same.* The gothic band Led Zeppelin in all their glory. Jimmy Page is dynamic and his speed up and down the fret board is awesome.

4. *The Last Waltz.* This features many superstars together in one film. Bob Dylan, Eric Clapton and a host of others join the Band in their final concert.

5. *The Buddy Holly Story.* An enjoyable film based on the life of one of the pioneers of rock. Many of his moves were

copied by later stars. Worth a look. Gary Bussey was nominated for an Academy Award for the title role.

6. *Let It Be.* Gives us the best look at the Beatles in performance. Their rooftop concert is a classic in spontaneity.

7. *No Nukes.* Worth the price of admission for Bruce Springsteen's performance. What can we say? The man is a mass of energy. Standing on top of the piano and then leaping to the stage and sliding across it on his knees—that has to be the best piece of gymnastics by a real guitarist we've ever seen.

8. *Sympathy for the Devil.* The Rolling Stones at their best; need we say more?

MTV

Cable TV has a station called MTV that is first rate. All the popular groups push their latest songs in a video format, which often features extraordinary air guitaring. Invaluable for novices and experts alike.

13. The Eight Best Air Guitar Albums

Great music is, of course, the most important ingredient for knock-down air guitar playing. Since everyone has his own

---

Neil Young air guitars with Joni Mitchell and Robbie Robertson in The Last Waltz.

heroes to pattern himself after, it is necessary to research this area yourself. We personally feel that the more dominant the rhythm and lead guitars, the better the air guitaring. In our national survey the albums most often played by today's air guitarists are:

1. *Get Yer Ya-Ya's Out.* The Rolling Stones in concert—crank it up! This album is excellent for air band workouts. Produced from in-concert tapes, the album includes ad-libs, audience banter, and equipment checks. The air guitarist can rip along with Keith Richard while the air vocalist can strut along with Mick Jagger. All the ingredients are here for hours (maybe years!) of air band interaction and hard-core fun. Though the "World's Greatest Rock 'n' Roll Band" has numerous albums (all very good), we heartily recommend this particular effort for serious air performers.

2. *Who's Next.* The Who have been an inspiration for air guitarists, vocalists, and drummers for two decades, so be prepared for action when you keep company with them on your stereo. This album (like their others) kicks veritable butt! A large playing area is recommended, preferably away from all breakables. Keith Moon's drum antics and Pete Townshend's guitar acrobatics should never be attempted by air performers under the influence of anything stronger than diet Seven-up. Don't worry—you can still play crisp and clean with no caffeine!

3. *Born to Run.* Bruce Springsteen is the ultimate model for an aspiring air guitarist. He sings lead vocals, plays lead guitar, and performs theatrically on stage. The *Born to Run* album captures Springsteen at his best. Play it loud. Learn the words. Learn the licks. Practice alone or with friends—the album provides material for air piano, organ, drums, bass, various horns, and even an air glockenspiel. Clarence Clemons' saxophone solos, by the way, are unparalleled in rock 'n' roll music.

4. *Damn the Torpedoes.* Tom Petty and his Heartbreakers provide a fine album for journeyman air musicians. Petty's tunes are extremely enjoyable, easily memorized, and can be duplicated confidently. The lead breaks can be tailored to confined playing areas. Play these songs in the living room for your folks. You can sedately entertain the whole family with this album, while maintaining your own rock 'n' roll integrity. Don't get us wrong—Petty's a rocker, but save your "duck walk" for the bedroom or the open stage.

5. *Essential Jimi Hendrix.* This collection of Hendrix hits gives you the "feel" of the man himself. Watch Hendrix in his movies, listen to the songs, and read about his incredible ability. But approach his style with a very controlled frenzy. Remember where it got him.

6. *The Eagles' Greatest Hits.* Many people consider the Eagles' music as "pop" or "soft-rock." Don't be fooled. This talented band provides air guitarists with some of the best stuff ever! Get a group together and try "Take It Easy." Impress your girl with your air rendition of "Peaceful Easy Feeling." While we particularly enjoy jumping into "Already Gone," we must admit to more than an occasional collision (and at least one broken nose) while getting together at the air mike for the chorus! So, play it—but play it safe.

7. *Van Halen II.* These guys are LOUD! All of their albums seem like they were produced specifically for air guitarists. (If they were, thanks!) While the mechanics of playing air guitars throughout *Van Halen II* aren't terribly outlandish, the acrobatics involved in duplicating their stage performance should only be attempted by expendable individuals. Also, don't practice near open windows *and* have a last will and testament in order.

8. *Anything by AC/DC.*

14. Advanced Techniques

Now that you know the basics about the origin and workings of this enjoyable instrument, here are several of the famous techniques used by some of the more popular guitarists of the last thirty or so years.

Duck Walk

The "Duck Walk," made famous by Chuck Berry in the mid-fifties, has become his trademark. It requires playing the guitar in an awkward squatting position, with one leg extended straight in front while the other leg supports the guitarist's weight (see example). The front leg is then raised and lowered in a bouncing motion as the performer hops across the stage. The performer may then turn around and repeat the procedure in the opposite direction. It is often advisable to walk back and forth across the stage in a simple squat or crouch, in order to limber up tight joints and come to terms with gravity. The Duck Walk is a very advanced technique and should not be attempted by anyone with weak ankles, or while under the influence of any mind-altering substance, or in the presence of male ducks.

The Duck Walk

Hours upon hours of practice are necessary to duck-walk this near the ground without permanently damaging your person or nearby possessions.

Windmill Method

The Windmill method is, of course, the tour de force of the Who's virtuoso guitarist Pete Townshend. It is a turbulent, space-consuming technique, so a broad area should be cleared before attempting it. No lamps, hanging plants, antiques, breakables, and definitely no chandeliers should be in the vicinity.

The feet should be planted firmly, at least shoulder's width apart. While playing the chords or notes normally with the left hand, the right arm is locked at the elbow and swung in an upward circular motion, pivoting at the shoulder (see illustration). The right hand crosses the guitar in time with the chords, and the effort is delivered with a vengeance that only a Who aficionado can comprehend. Any player with heavy metal or punk listening habits will insist the Windmill be a part of his repertoire.

As proficiency and confidence increase, the Windmill may be combined with a leap (à la Pete Townshend) for extra added flair. The legs can be either split or bent at the knees, and directed to the side or tucked behind the guitarist (see illustration). Any personal signature the air guitarist may add to this technique is optional, but it is imperative that the playing motion jives with the music. (It also helps if the player lands on his feet—unless serious bodily injury is his own personal trademark.)

Windmill Method

With friends, furniture, and fragiles out of the way, the windmill method can be continued until your hand turns purple. (Then change hands.)

Springsteen

The prime inspiration for our air guitar playing (and this humble book) has been Bruce Springsteen. His stage performances last more than three hours and are incredible to witness. We are emotionally and physically exhausted after just watching him! With the endurance of a marathon runner, he races across the stage, climbs all over his equipment, and leaps fearlessly into the crowd. He has taken everything from the roots of rock 'n' roll and incorporated it into these concerts. Springsteen joins past and present and makes all his moves look as if they were being executed for the first time. If you can capture that feeling in your own air guitar performances, you'll feel an exhilaration that is impossible to express in words.

One of Springsteen's patented techniques is the "Springsteen Slide." In this movement, the air guitarist runs frantically for at least a half dozen steps, then drops to his knees (at full speed) and slides to a halt. While sliding, the performer's back is arched, and the body and head lean back as far as prudence (or pain) allows. Needless to say, this technique requires a large area; halls are excellent (preferably sans carpeting). If practicing at home, merely remove any carpeting and buff or wax floors to a slick finish. If this is done while parents are out, your practice time is short and precious, so instill the same fervor and abandon into learning this technique that Bruce applies onstage.

Leaping Windmill

The intensity of effort is obvious in this air guitarist's expression. While airborne, legs can be manipulated in any direction physically possible. It helps if you land on your feet.

While the hall area may be convenient for practice, carpet removal, etc. may endanger your life (or at least your living arrangement with your parents!). Therefore, we offer an alternative—bowling alleys. While halls are excellent for practicing the Springsteen Slide, a bowling alley is PERFECT! Rent a lane (a minimal fee), rent some shoes (more minimal fee), and select a ball (no fee). So far, so good. Most bowling facilities have a juke box, so pre-select a few appropriate tunes (another small fee). However, since most juke boxes include very few Springsteen tunes, we suggest you bring along your own music—a "ghetto blaster" for instance. Once the tunes start, you're in business. So, to hell with the bowling. Start ripping up and down the alley, sliding on cue until you've mastered this colorful Springsteen maneuver. (If confronted by the alley's management, leave peacefully. There's always another bowling alley).

Sliding Springsteen

A perfectly executed "Sliding Springsteen" is its own reward. Even "The Boss" would be proud of this one.

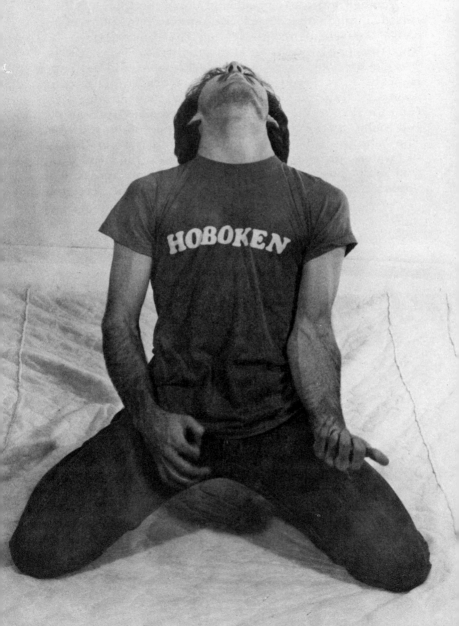

Another Springsteen trademark is the back-arched, heel-raised, guitar-extended leap he uses to end many of his songs. We call this technique the "Flying Springsteen." He leaps from one level of the stage to another. He leaps from the piano to the floor. He leaps from the PA speaker to the piano. He leaps . . . well you get the idea. These are all dazzling acrobatics, but you should begin from the beginning—leap from the floor *to* the floor. Work on style, posture, flair, etc. But mainly work on your landing; try to land on your *feet*. The technique is best illustrated by demonstration. If possible, watch Springsteen execute the leap during a concert. If that is not possible, a simple demonstration from any air guitarist who has studied Springsteen's repertoire can help.

Flying Springsteen

A maneuver only for experts, a "Flying Springsteen" is the perfect end to a hectic guitar set.

Jimi Hendrix

Anyone who has ever played a guitar or air guitar has been affected by Jimi Hendrix. His technique and innovation have been copied but never duplicated, even years after his death. Besides his use of feedback and distortion, his physical command of the guitar was incredible. One of his most famous playing techniques was to play the guitar behind his neck! He was also known for picking his guitar with his teeth. This incredible dexterity was complemented by his other moves, which are too numerous to mention here. Check out any of the many films *(Woodstock, Monterey Pop)* and books in which he is featured.

Author's note: Hendrix was apparently playing the air guitar *before* he learned to play the real thing. According to *Guitar Player* magazine, "Jimi received his first guitar—an inexpensive acoustic—from his father, who bought it after seeing his son holding the neck of a broom and strumming the bristles."

15. Partying

Now that you have the proper attire, and you have trained long and hard, it is time to reap the fruit of your labor—it's time to get down!

The requirements for an air guitar party are simple. The only things you need are: a) enough space on stage to accommodate your guests, b) a suitable stereo and music, c) guests, and d) a plentiful supply of air guitars.

A good icebreaker is a real electric guitar (not plugged in, of course). After getting other people up there jamming, discard the cumbersome electric guitar for the air guitar. As host courtesy dictates you should allow your guests to take some of the solos, as well as to choose some of the music.

Varying locations is a good idea for air guitar parties. During the summer months the beach is a great place; if you don't live near the beach, then a park is fine.

So, equipped with the knowledge that you attained by reading this book, the hours of practice should insure some fine parties.

16. The Air Masters

After years of practice and training, there are a few air guitarists who have learned all aspects of this art form. These elite are affectionately called Air Masters.

Believe it or not, they have reached a point where they can play every note on every instrument in the band, and even do it blindfolded! These few fanatics are a pure joy to behold. It is as if the actual band is in your living room for a private concert. They can be so realistic that people have actually asked them for their autographs! Incredible but true.

If you are dedicated enough, you might be able to join this rare breed.

17. Air Guitar Contests

Like other physical endeavors, some competitive-minded individuals believe that they are better than others and need recognition for their hours of practice.

Across the United States, air guitar competitions have sprung up in bars, nightclubs and on many college campuses. Since audience approval usually dictates the winners of these contests, we hope this book proves useful, not only to competitive air guitarists, but to the millions of audience members across the nation who cheer their favorite air musicians on to victory. Most of these untold millions are closet air guitarists themselves, who strum and pick their air guitars only privately whenever the urge strikes.

While musical tastes may vary, each of us has his own favorite music, his own favorite artists. Whether it's Michael Jackson or AC/DC, Bruce Springsteen or Kenny Rogers, Chuck Berry or Barry White, Frank Sinatra or Frank Zappa, each one has its own magic and mystique which excites you. You can turn on the radio and hear it; you can tune in MTV and see it; you can attend a concert and feel it. But when you push back your furniture, crank up your stereo, and pick up that air guitar, you can LIVE it!

"Well I got this guitar,
And I learned how to make it talk"

—Bruce Springsteen, "Thunder Road"